Copyright © 2014 Marshall Editions
Conceived, edited and designed by
Marshall Editions
Part of The Quarto Group
The Old Brewery,
6 Blundell Street,
London N7 9BH, UK

www.quarto.com

Pages 6–23, 33–39, and 62–65 written by John Farndon
Pages 24–32, 40–49, and 64–65 written by John Kelly
Pages 50–57, 60–61, and 66–77 written by Rob Beattie
Illustrators: Peter Bull, Steve Fricker, David Burnie,
Mike Harnden, John Kelly, Obin, Gary Smart
Editor: Vicky Egan
Designer: Jen Osborne
Art Director: Susi Martin
Publisher: Zeta Jones

ISBN: 978-1-78493-299-2

Printed and bound in China by 1010 Printing International Ltd
10 9 8 7 6 5 4 3 2 1   15 16 17 18 19 20

Words in **bold** can be found in the glossary on page 78.

CONTENTS

* INDICATES A GATEFOLD SECTION

INTRODUCTION

Two hundred years ago, if you wanted light, water or food in your home, you had to go and get it and carry it in yourself – unless you had servants to fetch it for you! Nowadays, you just flick a switch for light, turn on a tap for water and pick up your phone to get food delivered. It all seems so easy!

In this house, you can see some of the things that we often take for granted in our homes. But just how do they work? That's what the little people in this book will show you.

Words that need further explanation are in **bold** and can be found on pages 78-79.

Turning on the light to read a newspaper or a letter

Flushing away water from the toilet

Soaking in a bath full of hot water, or taking a refreshing shower

Cooking, doing the washing, washing dishes or having a drink of fresh water

Throwing all the rubbish into the bin

Sewer

Water pipe

Satellite dish

SOMETHING IN THE AIR

Television and radio programmes arrive at your house as invisible signals in the air. A specially shaped metal tube called an aerial picks up these signals. A radio aerial is either on top of the radio or inside it. Television signals can be picked up by a big TV aerial on the roof or by a satellite dish on the wall. They can also come into the house through an underground cable.

BE CAREFUL!

Electricity and gas can be dangerous if not used properly. Always check with an adult before touching electrical equipment, and never use a cooker without an adult's help. Be careful, too, when you turn on the hot tap – the water may be very hot!

BURROWING IN

Water and gas come into your home through pipes buried in the ground, and electricity comes through cables containing copper wire. The telephone lines may also enter by an underground cable. Sewage and waste water are taken away from the house by a big drain called a sewer.

KNOCK, KNOCK!

When friends come to visit, they may fly by jet to the nearest airport and then take a train, or they may hire a car and use satellite navigation to find your house.

Sending messages by computer or talking on the telephone or on your mobile to a friend far away

Watching cartoons on television

Ordering things by telephone

Turning on the heating to keep the house nice and warm

Electricity cable

Gas pipe

Telephone line

ELECTRICITY

When you turn on a lamp, an amazing invisible energy called electricity makes the lamp glow with light. Electricity is made, or generated, in a power station. But how does it get from the power station to the lamp in your house?

Hydroelectric power

Coal, oil and gas power

Nuclear power

1 GETTING TO STEAM

Power stations burn coal, oil, gas or **nuclear fuel** to boil water into steam. The steam rushes along pipes and hits the blades of a wheel called a **turbine**, whirling it around fast. In **hydroelectric stations**, water rushing down from a dam spins the turbine.

Rushing water   *Jet of steam*

2 GOING FOR A SPIN

As the turbine spins, it turns a coil of copper wire between the poles of a huge **magnet**. This is a **generator**.

Magnet

Coil of copper wire

Turbine blades spin round at high speed

The shaft of the turbine is linked to a generator

Step-up transformer

3 MAKING CURRENTS

The magnet's power drags tiny energy bundles, called **electrons**, through the wire. The electrons form a flow of electricity called an electric **current**.

4 RAISING THE CURRENT

The current from the power station is too weak to reach your house. Its strength is raised, or stepped up, by sending it through an iron ring called a **transformer**.

A big wire picks up the electricity from the coil

Meter

Fuse box

Electric kettle

Plug in socket

Television

Washing machine

Electric lamp

8 SAFETY WIRE

Inside your home, a **meter** measures how much electricity you use. You'll also find a row of **fuses** – thin wires that melt if the current reaches dangerous levels. This stops the current from flowing.

9 PLUGGING INTO POWER

Electricity flows around your house through wires called ring mains, which are hidden under the floor or in the wall. Sockets let you tap into the electricity in the ring main. When you plug your lamp into the socket and turn it on - zap! - instant power!

Ring main

Electric mains

Step-down transformer

7 TAKE YOUR SHARE

The stepped-down current is then fed into cables called electric **mains**, which run beneath the streets. Other cables branch off from the mains and go into every house, factory or office. They deliver the electricity to wherever it is needed.

6 TRANSFORMING THE CURRENT

A powerful current is needed to send electricity over long distances. When the electricity reaches your town, the current is reduced, or stepped down, by another transformer.

Pylon

High-power cables

5 SAFETY FIRST

The strong, stepped-up current is dangerous. It is carried in huge cables buried safely underground or strung between tall pylons.

Buried cable

GAS

The gas used by gas cookers and central heating systems is not just any old gas. It is called natural gas, because it forms naturally under the ground. Natural gas is very flammable, which means that it bursts into flame easily. So how does this dangerous gas get safely to your home?

Geologists looking for gas

Gas platform

Drill

3 TIME TO DRILL

When gas is found, a huge platform is built above the rock where the gas is trapped. A giant drill tunnels into the ocean floor and taps into the gas pocket. The gas is then pumped ashore through pipes, and is cleaned.

1 LOOKING FOR GAS

You can tell if a tin can is full by listening to the sound it makes when you tap it. Geologists find gas in a similar way. They make explosions underwater, and then listen to the vibrations that travel through the rocks under the ocean floor. This tells them if any gas is trapped in hollows in the rock.

2 OLD BONES

Gas forms from the bones and shells of dead sea creatures buried under layers of sand, mud and rock. Over millions of years, the massive weight of the sand, mud and rock changes the bones and shells into natural gas.

Pipes are put into the drill holes to suck out the gas

5 MAKING THE GAS PURE

Squeezing and cooling the gas turns it into a liquid. As it warms up, it turns back into a gas and separates from its impurities, which remain liquid.

Squeezing

Cleaning the gas

Cooling

4 AT THE CLEANERS

Once on shore, the gas is sent to an extraction unit. Here, it is filtered to remove unwanted dust, sulphur and water.

6 WHAT'S THAT SMELL?

Natural gas has no smell. A smell is added so you can detect gas leaks.

7 GO GAS

Now the pure gas (with added smell) is pumped through pipes at about 26 kilometres per hour. The gas may need to be sent long distances, so there are extra pumps, called compressor stations, along the way to keep it going.

Squeezing the gas

Cooling the gas

Compressor station

Hot-water boiler

8 GAS STORE

People use different amounts of gas from day to day and from season to season. Any gas that is not needed immediately is stored in tanks or pumped into giant underground caverns.

10 BURN IT!

Finally, the gas is piped to your house. A meter records how much gas you burn as you heat the water, cook or run your gas central heating.

9 LIQUID SUPPLY

Natural gas is stored as a liquid, because this takes up less space. To change it into a liquid, the gas is squeezed and cooled.

Gas is released when needed

Gas central heating

Gas stove

Gas meter

11

WATER

Turn on the tap and out comes water – clean, fresh and ready for drinking, washing and bathing in. In the Australia, around 200 litres of water are used per day by every person. Nearly all of this water starts as rain, but how does it reach your taps?

Filtering the water

Pumping rainwater through pipes

1 REFRESHING RAIN

Rain runs into rivers or sinks into the ground. Pumps suck this water up into huge pipes, and any objects in the water, such as twigs or dead fish, are filtered out.

8 BATH TIME

The water mains are joined to small pipes in your house. The pipes go to a storage tank or straight to the taps. Turn on the tap, and out gushes water!

Water for drinking

Water for bathing

7 WHOOSH!

Some streets have special taps, called fire hydrants, on the pavement. These connect straight to the mains, where water flows under very high pressure. This means that when firefighters attach a hose to a fire hydrant, they get a very strong jet of water for putting out fires.

Water for washing the dishes

Water for fighting fires

3 FLOCS AWAY

The chemicals are mixed in thoroughly. At this stage, the water still has small pieces of dirt in it. Adding the chemicals makes all of the tiny specks of dirt bunch together into lumps called **flocs**. The flocs are no bigger than grains of salt, but they are heavy enough to start slowly sinking.

Adding chemicals

2 DIRTY WATER

Rainwater is usually dirty, so it must be cleaned, or treated, before we can use it in our homes. First, two chemicals, aluminium sulphate and lime, are added to the water.

Mixing in chemicals

6 WATER BANK

The water is now safe to drink. It is piped through huge tubes, called conduits, to covered **reservoirs** or to tanks at the top of water towers, where it is stored until it is needed. When people turn on their taps, the water runs into big pipes called mains, and from there it is pumped to their houses.

4 SETTLING DOWN

The water then goes to a **sedimentation tank**, where the flocs sink to the bottom and form a thick sludge. The sludge is removed, and the water goes on to the next stage.

Filtration tank

Water flows into mains

Fire hydrant

5 A REAL STRAIN

The water is still not quite clean, so it has to be drained through layers of sand and small stones that trap very fine dirt. This process is called filtration. Special germs called bacteria are added to eat up any tiny living creatures left in the water. Finally, a little bleach is added to kill off the germs. Clean water at last!

SEWAGE

When you pull the plug in the bath or flush the toilet, all the water and waste goes down the drain. But where does it go from there, and why doesn't the world just get smellier and smellier?

Away it goes!

6 THE FILTER BEDS

The dirty water is sprinkled onto the **filter beds**, which are made up of layers of slimy stones.

Filter beds

Steam from the boiling water powers the pumps in the sewage treatment plant

Methane from the sludge is burned to boil water

7 HELPFUL GERMS

The slime on the stones contains **bacteria**. These eat up any harmful material left in the water as it trickles down through the layers of stones.

Sludge digestion tank

Clean sludge from the digestion tank may be used as manure

1 DOWN THE DRAIN

The used water that goes down the drain flows into a tunnel called a sewer – which is why the waste is called sewage. Sewers are so big that sewage flows through them like an underground river.

2 GOING PLACES

The sewer carries all of the sewage from homes, offices, restaurants and factories in your local area to a sewage treatment plant.

Once it has been cleaned and dried, grit from sewage is used to repair holes in the road.

Filtering out large objects

4 SETTLING DOWN

The sewage is left to stand for a while in a large tank. Here, solid material sinks to the bottom and forms a muddy **sludge**. The remaining liquid is pumped away for cleaning in the filter beds.

Grease floats to the surface and is carefully skimmed off

3 GOOD GRILLING

At the treatment plant, the sewage passes through a filter that traps rags, rubbish and any large objects. Any grit (small stones and sand) in the sewage settles in grit traps and is removed.

Grit trap

The grit is washed and dried for use in building work

5 SLUDGE

The sludge goes to a **sludge digestion tank**, where bacteria feed on it and release a gas called methane.

Sludge settles in the tank

8 CLEAN WATER

The sewage from your house has been changed back into clean water. The clean water is pumped from the sewage plant into rivers or out to sea.

RUBBISH

When you put out the rubbish, do you ever wonder what happens to it? Some things can be **recycled** and used again, but others have to be buried or burned.

PLASTIC

Most types of plastic do not rot, so rubbish dumps are being piled higher and higher with old plastics.

METAL

Many metal objects, such as aluminium drinks cans and steel food tins, can be recycled.

GLASS

Glass jars and bottles can be recycled, but first they must be separated into different colours.

PAPER

Although thousands of trees are cut down each year to make new books and magazines, most paper can be recycled.

The plastics are crushed before being recyled.

The metals are sorted and cleaned.

The glass is smashed into little pieces.

Wastepaper must be chopped very finely before it can be recycled

The crushed plastics are melted and put into moulds to make new objects.

Each type of metal is heated until it melts, and then poured into moulds.

Smashed glass of each colour is melted down to make new glass of that colour.

Scraps of paper are mixed with water and boiled to make a pulp.

The pulp is spread over a wire mesh, and squeezed dry to make new paper

Unloading the rubbish

1 COLLECTING RUBBISH

Refuse trucks collect any rubbish that can't be recycled. They take it to rubbish dumps, or to **incinerators** to be burned.

2 AT THE DUMP

The rubbish is crushed to make it as small as possible. Then it is dumped into huge holes or pits in the ground, called landfill sites.

4 NEW LAND

When the hole is full, the site is covered over. Once all the dangerous gases have been removed, the site can be used for something else.

Each layer of rubbish is covered with a layer of soil

3 HUGE PILE-UP

After being dumped in a hole, the crushed rubbish is packed down tight. As it rots, it gives off explosive gases that can be dangerous if allowed to build up. Pipes are built next to the hole, so the gases can be collected or burned off.

17

LARGE LETTERS

The letters move along a conveyor belt

MEDIUM LETTERS

Sorting office

SMALL LETTERS

Sizing the letters

Reading the address and postcode

1 LARGE, MEDIUM OR SMALL?

The postal worker takes the letters to a sorting office. Here, a conveyor belt carries them to a **sizing machine**. This separates the post into small, medium and large letters. One machine checks the letters have stamps, while another prints a postmark showing where and when they were posted.

11 LAST RE-SORT

At last, your letter reaches the town it is addressed to. Here, at the local post office, the letters are sorted again – this time into individual districts and streets. The post is now ready for delivery.

Each mailbag contains all the letters for a particular district

10 GOING UP COUNTRY

If a letter is going to a town nearby, it will be sent in a truck or van. Post for places farther away is sometimes sent by train. But in very large countries, letters may have to be put on another plane that will carry them to towns on the other side of the country.

Delivery of letters to towns and cities begins

OFF WE GO...

Once your letter has been dropped into a postbox, it's time for the postal service to start its work. There are different collection times throughout the day, so your letter may sit in the dark for a while until a postal worker comes along and collects it from the postbox.

Collecting the post

Letters in a postbox

Your letter has finally arrived!

12 INTO THE MAILBOX

The mailbag contains post for homes and businesses. Each postal worker is given all of the letters for a small district. Some of them deliver letters by truck or van, while others deliver them by bicycle. But most postal workers deliver their letters on foot.

It can take as little as two days for your letter to travel halfway around the world to Australia

SENDING MAIL

When you send a letter from New York City, in the United States, to Sydney, Australia, it somehow manages to find its way to the right address. Lift these pages to find out what happens.

THE RIGHT ADDRESS

Your letter won't reach its destination without the right address and **postcode** on the envelope. Each section of a street has a postcode – a sequence of letters and numbers. These help machines to sort the letters so they go to the right places.

HOW DOES THIS LETTER FROM THE USA GET TO

If you don't have any relatives or friends living abroad, ask your parents or teacher to help you find a pen-pal overseas.

If you're writing a business letter, you may end it with "Yours sincerely", and then your full name.

If you're writing to a friend, you may end your letter with "from" or "love from", and then your name.

If you're writing to a friend, you may begin your letter with "Dear", and then your friends name.

Put your own address at the top of the letter so that the person you're writing to knows where to send the reply. Include the date, too.

18

DELIVERED TO THE DOOR

It's exciting to receive a letter, especially when it comes from far away. Here, your letter is being opened in Sydney after it has travelled halfway round the world.

STAMPS

Your letter won't be delivered unless it has the correct stamp. Sending a letter abroad usually costs more than sending it to someone in your own country.

Each country has its own stamps.

People often save special letters for many years.

Postmark shows where and when the letter was posted

AUSTRALIA ON THE OTHER SIDE OF THE WORLD?

North America

New York

Europe

Asia

Timbuktu

Atlantic Ocean

Africa

South America

Pacific Ocean

Australia

Sydney

You can send a letter anywhere in the world – but it can take a long time to get to remote places, such as Timbuktu in Africa's Sahara Desert.

4 LETTER SORTING

In the sorting office, there is a separate mailbag or box for each city or foreign country. A bar code reader reads the bar code printed on your letter, and drops it into the mailbox for all international post.

5 HIGH-FLYING MAIL

A big truck takes all the boxes and bags destined for Australia to the airport, where they are loaded onto an aeroplane. Some large items are sent overseas by ship, but most post is sent by airmail because planes are much faster than ships.

Sorting the post for each city and country

Take-off!

Airmail is carried by plane to faraway places

The plane takes more than 12 hours to reach Australia from the United States

7 MIDSUMMER MAIL

It was midwinter in the U.S. when the letter was posted, but when the plane lands in Australia, it is midsummer! This is because the southern half of the world has its seasons exactly six months after the northern half.

Unloading the post

6 LOSING A DAY

Sydney is 14 hours ahead of New York, so during the long flight, the pilot has to put the calendar forward one day.

2 WHERE TO?

A machine called an **optical character reader** scans the writing on the front of the envelope to work out where your letter is going. It tells another machine, called a bar code printer, where that is.

Printing the bar code

3 BAR CODE

The bar code printer prints a row of thick and thin bars, known as a bar code, on your letter to show where it is going. Only machines called bar code readers can understand this code.

BAR CODE PRINTER

Reading the bar codes

9 WHERE TO NOW?

A bar code reader scans the barcodes on the letters to find out where they are going. It then drops each letter into a mailbag or box for the right place.

Letters are sorted into mailboxes for the different cities

SYDNEY

ALICE SPRINGS

MELBOURNE

8 DOWN UNDER

The post is unloaded from the plane and taken by truck to another sorting office. Now the letter is in the hands of the Australian postal service.

Sorting office in Australia

MICROWAVE OVEN

A microwave oven heats food in a fraction of the time it takes a conventional oven, and the oven itself doesn't get hot. Using a device called a magnetron, it fires a powerful form of energy known as **microwaves.**

WHAT ARE MICROWAVES?

Microwaves travel at 300,000 kilometres per second, and can pass through air, food or empty space. Microwaves from space hit us all the time, but they are so weak that they have no effect on us. The energy used in microwave ovens is much more powerful.

COOKING WITH WAVES

When microwave energy passes through the water **molecules** in food, the molecules begin to move rapidly. This movement produces heat, which cooks the food.

1 COLD

In cold food, water molecules are spread out randomly. They move about, but only slowly.

2 WARM

As microwaves travel through the food, the water molecules move rapidly in different directions.

3 HOT

The rapidly moving molecules produce heat, which spreads through the food and cooks it.

4 INSIDE OUT

The microwaves enter the food and cause it to heat up, so it cooks from the inside out. A conventional oven, by contrast, heats the air around the food.

Inner lining

3 SCATTERING THE WAVES

Microwaves cannot travel through metal, so they bounce off the fan blades and shoot off in all directions around the oven.

Rotating fan blade

Reflected microwave beam

2 CREATING MICROWAVES

When you press the power button, a magnetron uses electricity to produce a beam of microwaves. This beam travels across the top of the oven and hits a rotating metal fan.

Microwaves leaving magnetron

Electric motor drives fan and food turntable

Drive belt

Turntable rotates slowly to ensure food cooks evenly

Timer can be set to minutes and seconds

Push to start

5 A PROTECTIVE LAYER

The oven is lined to prevent microwaves from leaking out, which would waste energy. Leaked microwaves could also be harmful to anyone standing near the oven.

1 QUICK TIME

Before pushing the power button to start the machine, you must set the timer. Microwaves cook food very quickly, so it's important to get the timing just right.

REFRIGERATOR

A refrigerator is a very important machine because keeping food cold stops it from going off. Normally you never see the back of a fridge, but this one has been turned around so you can see all its working parts.

A fridge works by taking heat from the inside compartment and carrying it to the outside. It does this by continuously pumping a special fluid, called a refrigerant, through a long loop of piping. On its journey, the refrigerant changes from a liquid into a **vapour**, and back to a liquid. As it becomes a vapour, the fridge absorbs heat from the food. When it turns back into a liquid, it releases the heat into the kitchen.

1 KEEPING COOL

If you go for a swim and then come out without drying off, you'll soon start to feel cold. This is because the water on your skin, warmed by your body, starts to **evaporate** (turn to vapour) and takes heat away from you. In the same way, a fridge becomes cold as the heat from inside it turns liquid refrigerant into vapour.

BAD NEWS FOR GERMS

All food has some germs on it. In warm conditions, these germs grow quickly and can make food go off. In a cool fridge they grow more slowly, so food stays fresh for longer.

2 INTO THE INTERIOR

When the refrigerant enters the freezer, it moves through a narrow **nozzle** into a series of pipes. Inside these pipes, the liquid refrigerant absorbs any heat from inside the freezer, and expands into a vapour. The freezer cools down, and its contents become very cold.

3 BACK TO THE COMPRESSOR

The refrigerant then flows out of the freezer, carrying heat absorbed from the food. Next it travels down to the **compressor** (a small pump), which applies **pressure** to the vaporized refrigerant. The refrigerant is squeezed back into liquid form, and begins to release heat.

Liquid refrigerant expands into these pipes and becomes a vapour

Narrow nozzle, or expansion valve

Freezer

Insulating layer between the hot pipes and the cool refrigerator

Refrigerant from freezer flows down to the compressor

Compressor, powered by an electric motor

Electric motor

Thermostat

Refrigerant condenses (turns into a liquid) inside this pipe (the condenser)

Heat spreads through metal rods into the air

4 HEAT LOSS

After passing through the compressor, the refrigerant zigzags its way across the back of the refrigerator through another pipe. During this part of its journey, pressure from the compressor continues to turn the vaporized refrigerant into a liquid. This releases the heat that was absorbed in the freezer. The heat travels away from the pipe, through metal rods, and escapes into the air outside the refrigerator.

5 STAYING AT THE RIGHT TEMPERATURE

The compressor is controlled by a thermostat – a device that regulates temperature. The compressor starts pumping when the refrigerator's temperature starts to rise, and stops when the refrigerator cools to the desired degree.

27

WASHING MACHINE

People used to wash clothes by hand, using rocks from rivers to scrub out the dirt. Technology has made this chore much easier, but what happens to the clothes is still quite similar. Using drums, springs, belts, **bearings** and, of course, detergent, the modern washing machine removes the grime from your clothes and then spins them until they are almost dry. The machine follows special programmes that take the clothes through cycles of soaking, washing and rinsing, until finally they are ready to be put in a tumble dryer or hung on a washing line to dry.

1 CHOOSING YOUR WASH

The control panel lets you select the right wash programme for your clothes. Some fabrics are much more delicate than others, and need a gentler wash. Each programme sets the length of the wash cycle, the speed at which the inner drum spins and the temperature of the water.

2 CHEMICAL CLEANERS

Before you start the machine, you need to put some detergent into it. Detergents contain more than a dozen ingredients. Some help the water to soak into clothes, while others remove stains and dirt. Many detergents also contain **enzymes** – chemicals that help break down substances, such as fat or blood, on your clothes.

3 GETTING GOING

The washing machine is driven by an electric motor. (You can find out more about electric motors on page 47).

4 THE DRUM KIT

The motor is conntected by a drive belt to the inner drum. When you switch on the machine, the drive belt turns the inner drum, which rotates on ball bearings. The drum is full of holes that allow water to flow into and out of the washing. As the drum rotates, the clothes move against each other, as well as against the sides of the drum, and it is this agitation, with help from the detergent, that removes the dirt from the clothing. The outer drum cannot move, and forms a watertight compartment when the door is closed.

Rubber seal

Detergent drawer

Safety lock prevents door being opened while machine is switched on

Box of detergent

5 GETTING RID OF WATER

Although water flows into the washing machine under its own pressure, once it is no longer needed, it must be pumped out. A pump draws the dirty water from the outer drum and through a filter, before finally squirting it into the waste pipe.

6 SPRING LOADED

After the water has been removed, the machine spin dries the clothes. The inner drum can whirl around at more than 1,000 revolutions per minute. If the clothes are unevenly spread out, this creates powerful vibrations. Heavy-duty springs absorb most of this movement, but built-in weights are also needed to prevent the machine from shaking itself to pieces.

Water intake pipe

Weights prevent vibrations from moving the machine

Srpings absorb vibrations

Drive belt

Ball bearings allow the inner drum to spin freely

Stainless steel inner drum with holes

Watertight outer drum

Thermostat

Heating element controlled by the thermostat heats water to the right temperature

Water drains through holes in inner drum

Motor

Pump

Filter removes grit and fibres before waste water reaches the pump

TOASTER

For breakfast lovers, this could be one of the most important machines ever invented. It toasts bread to perfection and automatically turns off when the slices are ready to eat. This cut-away toaster will help answer one of the most pressing questions facing any toast enthusiast. How does the toaster know when the toast is done? The answer lies in a tiny device called a bimetallic strip, which responds to heat by changing shape. The strip is set to release a catch at just the right moment, popping up the toast and preventing it from burning.

1 TURNING ON THE HEAT

Bread is toasted by electric elements that are backed by a heat-resistant shield. The shield keeps the case from getting hot by reflecting heat back toward the toast.

6 READY FOR LIFT OFF

When you put bread in the toaster and push down the handle, you stretch a pair of metal springs. This causes a catch near the handle to engage with a hinged metal bar, and the bread is held in position. When the toast is ready, the metal bar is released, the spring contracts, and the toast shoots skyward.

5 TIMED TO PERFECTION

Some toasters are controlled by a timer instead of a bimetallic strip. When the timer reaches zero, it activates a switch that turns on the electromagnet. (To find out more about electromagnets see page 58).

4 TRIPPING THE CATCH

When electricity flows through the toaster's wire coils, it produces a powerful magnetic field. The field attracts a metal catch, and when this catch moves, it releases the lever that holds the toast down.

Handle stretches spring when pulled down.

3 AS YOU LIKE IT

The browning control adjusts the distance between the bimetallic strip and the metal contact. The greater the distance, the more the strip has to bend, and the browner the toast becomes.

Browning adjustment rod.

Hinged catch keeps spring from contracting and can be disengaged by electromagnet.

Electromagnet

Hinged metal bar holds toast down until catch disengages.

Powerful spring engages catch when handle is pulled down.

Electric elements become red hot as electricity passes through them.

Bimetallic strip bends as it expands – when it touches the electrical contact, the circuit is completed.

2 BENDING WITH THE HEAT

The small bimetallic strip is a vital part of the toaster. It is made of two different metals sandwiched together. As the toaster heats up, one of the metals expands more than the other, causing the strip to bend. Eventually, the strip bends so much that it touches an electrical contact. This allows current to flow into the wires around the electromagnet, which in turn activates the release catch.

FOOD PROCESSOR

When preparing food by hand, many jobs – such as grating cheese, mixing batter or slicing carrots – can take a long time. A food processor can do the work much more quickly and efficiently. Food can be chopped, liquidized, kneaded, mixed or sliced in seconds!

A simple device on the lid of the processor prevents accidents from happening. The lid has a catch that connects to a safety switch. If the lid is on and fastened tightly, the switch allows electricity to flow through the motor. But if the lid has been removed, or if it is not positioned correctly, the motor will not turn on.

Speed control

Power supply

POWER ON

A food processor uses an electric motor to make things move. The motor produces only about one-hundredth of the power of a car's engine, but this is enough to chop up almost any food.

CONTROLLING THE SPEED

The speed of the motor is determined by the strength of the electric current flowing through it. When the control knob is set at the slowest speed, only a weak current flows through the motor. At the highest speed, the current is stronger and the motor moves more rapidly.

Drive belt

Food chute in lid

SPECIAL TOOLS FOR DIFFERENT TASKS

A food processor is supplied with a range of attachments for chopping, slicing or blending different kinds of foods.

WHISK

The whisk contains a set of **gears** that makes the two whisk blades turn quickly. As the blades spin, they fold air into the food. The whisk is used to whip cream or egg whites.

Gears

Blade

KNEADER

This attachment turns slowly, beating a flour and liquid mixture to make dough. The kneader is also used for folding ingredients into one another.

Bowl

Axle

Turning wheel attached to axle

Chopping blades attached to axle

MIX IT UP!

If you want to mix, chop or whisk lots of ingredients together at once, you can put the foods straight into the bowl, put on the lid and turn on the power. You can also add ingredients a little at a time while the motor is running by dropping them down a food chute in the lid. This means you don't have to keep stopping the motor, and your fingers are protected.

PIZZA TIME

You might find it annoying to have to wait an hour to get your pizza, but it actually takes about a year to grow and collect all the ingredients.

1 MADE TO ORDER

As soon as you call the pizzeria with your order, the pizza chefs jump into action. First, they mix yeast, sugar, water and a little flour. Then they leave the mixture to settle.

Yeast

Flour

Water

Getting the ingredients from the store

Sugar

3 BUBBLE POWER

Next, the mixture is poured into a bowl with olive oil, some salt and more flour, to make a dough. The bubbles are like millions of tiny balloons. They make the dough light and airy. Without the gas bubbles, the pizza dough would be thick and heavy.

2 GETTING FROTHY

Yeast makes the sugar **ferment**. This means that the sugar turns into alcohol and releases bubbles of a gas called carbon dioxide, which make the mixture frothy.

The yeast mixture ferments

Yeast mixture

Olive oil

Salt

Flour

4 KNEADING TIME

The dough is placed on a board, and the chef kneads it, pushing and squeezing it into a smooth lump.

Dough

Mixing the ingredients for the dough

Kneading the dough

INGREDIENTS FOR THE PIZZA BASE

WHEAT

Wheat is grown from seed and cut when it is ripe.

Threshing

Winnowing shakes the grains out of their husks.

The grain is milled (ground) to make a fine powder – in the past, heavy stones were used. The powder is the flour used to make the pizza base.

SALT

Salt is found under the ground. Huge blocks of it are cut at salt mines.

The blocks of salt are ground up, and the tiny salt crystals are then dried and packed.

At the pizzeria, the salt is poured into salt pots, ready for use.

YEAST

Yeast is a fungus. It is grown in warm tubs, or vats.

When it's ready, the yeast is removed from the vats, dried and cut into chunks, called cakes.

The dried yeast cakes are then wrapped, ready for sale.

OLIVE OIL

Olives grow on trees in some warm countries.

They are picked from the trees and then squeezed in a screw press.

All of the juice runs out of the olives and is collected in bottles. The juice is called olive oil.

The olive oil is delivered to the pizzeria.

SUGAR

Sugar comes from a plant called sugarcane. When the cane is ripe, it is cut.

The sugarcane is crushed to extract the juice. This is boiled until the water in the juice has evaporated, leaving behind sugar crystals.

Blocks of sugar crystals are cut into cubes.

MAKING A PIZZA

In many parts of the world, you can have a ready-to-eat meal delivered straight to your door simply by making a telephone call. When you order a pizza, for example, the pizzeria somehow manages to get together ingredients from all over the world and send you a freshly cooked pizza in less than an hour. Lift these pages to see just how it's done.

HUNGRY WORLD

In the past, most people lived on food that was grown and produced locally. This is still true in many parts of the world, especially in rural areas far from big cities. But in places such as North America, Europe, Japan and Australia people can eat foods from all over the world. Your breakfast glass of orange juice may come from Florida in the United States, the wheat for your bread may come from India, the butter from New Zealand and the apricots in the jam may be Spanish!

HOW DOES A PIZZERIA DELIVER A PIZZA SO QUICKLY?

WHAT SHALL WE HAVE?

You can get so many different types of food delivered to your door that choosing what to have can be a real challenge! Besides pizzas, there are Indian curries, Chinese stir-fries, American burgers, Italian pasta, and so on. We've decided on a cheese and tomato pizza, with extra anchovies. If you don't like what we've chosen, don't worry – there are many more dishes on the menu!

Cheese & Tomato
Vegetarian Deluxe
Seafood Splash
Ham & Mushroom
Chunky Chicken
Hot & Spicy
Meat Mountain
Cheese Feast

Just looking at the menu makes your mouth water, doesn't it? So get on the phone right away and place your order.

34

WHAT'S IN IT FOR US?

Apart from being very tasty, our pizza is full of useful things. Tomatoes, cheese, yeast, wheat and anchovies contain vitamins, which our bodies need to work properly and stay healthy.

The wheat in the pizza base contains carbohydrates, which give our bodies energy to keep us going

Anchovies and cheese contain proteins, which our bodies need to grow and to repair themselves

Optional extra: mushrooms. These contain vitamins that give us energy and help our body to resist allergies

Cheese and olive oil contain fats, which our bodies use to store energy

WHERE IN THE WORLD DOES IT ALL COME FROM?

The ingredients for our pizza are: wheat, yeast, sugar, tomatoes, salt, olive oil, mozzarella cheese and anchovies (with optional mushrooms). This map shows you the main areas where the ingredients come from, except for yeast, which is made in many parts of the world.

KEY

- Wheat
- Sugar
- Tomatoes
- Salt
- Olive oil
- Mozzarella cheese
- Anchovies

North America

Atlantic Ocean

Europe

Asia

Africa

South America

Pacific Ocean

Australia

35

11 DOORSTEP DELIGHT

The doorbell rings. It's the driver with your order. You open the carton and there is your favourite pizza – hot, fresh and ready to eat. Enjoy your meal!

Pizza's here!

Oh boy!

I'm hungry!

TOPPING INGREDIENTS

The curds are separated from the whey and pressed into a mould, where they are left to turn into cheese.

The egg-shaped lumps of cheese are usually sold in plastic bags full of water to keep them fresh.

As the milk curdles, it forms solid curds and liquid whey.

MOZZARELLA CHEESE

Cow's milk is heated to kill any germs.

TOMATOES

Tomatoes are picked from vines when they are ripe.

They are cooked and strained, and may be beaten to make a pulp.

Machines heat the pulp to make a paste, which is sealed in tins.

ANCHOVIES

Anchovies are caught at sea in nets with tiny holes. The fish are taken to fish factories, where they are cut up and boned.

Fish factory

The fish are put in tins.

Vegetable oil or olive oil is added to keep the fish moist and fresh.

9 ALL CUT UP

The pizza chef lays the pizza in a carton and cuts it into slices using a special pizza cutter, which is shaped like a wheel with a jagged edge. Can you smell it now?

10 PIZZA TO GO!

A driver packs up your pizza. He or she checks your address and delivers the pizza to your door.

8 HOT PIZZA

When the pizza comes out of the oven, the base is cooked just right, and the topping is piping hot.

The pizza needs only 8 to 15 minutes in the oven.

7 GET COOKING!

Pizzas are usually baked in special ovens that ensure they cook evenly all the way through. The bubbles in the dough grow as they get warmer, making the pizza fatter and lighter.

Ready for the oven

6 TOPPING SHOW

Most pizza toppings start with a coating of tomato paste. Mozzarella cheese and anchovies are also added to this pizza.

Tomato paste

Anchovy slices

Mozzarella cheese

Now that the base is ready, the topping can go on.

5 SPIN A DISC

When the dough is ready, it is spun into a disc shape. An expert pizza chef can spin it on one finger!

38

VACUUM CLEANER

Twenty-four hours a day, an invisible blizzard piles up dust inside our homes. Some of the dust blows in when we open doors or windows, but a lot of it comes from tiny fibres that break away from our clothes, and microscopic flakes that wear away from the surface of our skin. If dust is not cleaned away, it quickly builds up on surfaces all over the house. Fortunately, there is an easy way to get rid of it. The vacuum cleaner creates **suction** that collects these particles of dust, packing them into a bag that can then be thrown away.

④ CLEANING BY SUCTION

The dust bag is in a compartment in the upper part of the vacuum cleaner, along with a filter. The compartment is airtight, but the dust bag contains tiny holes that let air flow through to a fan underneath. When the cleaner is switched on, the fan sucks air out of the compartment, producing a partial vacuum. The resulting suction pulls air and dirt through the dust pipe into the dust bag.

Disposable dust bag traps dirt and dust while allowing air to pass through

Fan sucks air out of airtight compartment

③ DUST ON THE MOVE

Once the dust has been dislodged from the carpet, it is sucked into a pipe. The pipe carries it through the machine and into the dust bag.

⑥ A BAGFUL OF DUST

The dust bag is made of a special material that allows air to flow through while keeping dust and dirt inside. As the bag fills with dust and dirt, it becomes more difficult for air to flow through. As a result, there is less suction and the vacuum does not clean as well.

⑤ FULL OF DIRT?

Each time the vacuum cleaner is turned on, the dust bag swells up like a balloon. This is because the pressure of the air inside the bag becomes greater than the **air pressure** around it.

On-off switch

Airtight compartment

Dust pipe

A second filter ensures that all the dust and dirt is removed before the air leaves the

Hinged door for removing filter

The electric motor uses as much energy as ten standard light bulbs

1 THE BIG BRUSH-OFF

Dust and dirt often work their way deep into a carpet, where they are difficult to dislodge. A vacuum cleaner has brushes that sweep them from the carpet and into the air. Once the particles are airborne, they can be sucked into the machine.

2 PORTABLE POWER

An electric motor powers the rotating brushes and the fan that sucks air through the machine.

Drive belt

Brushes are attached to a rotating axle

Air in dust bag

Partial vacuum

Fan

Air outside

WHAT IS A VACUUM?

A roomful of air contains billions of tiny particles known as **atoms**. These are constantly spreading themselves evenly to fill all the space around them. A vacuum contains no atoms at all. There is no such thing as a true vacuum, because some atoms are present everywhere, but a partial vacuum can be created by a vacuum cleaner. In a partial vacuum, there are fewer atoms than in the surrounding air, which will immediately rush in to equalize the pressure. In a vacuum cleaner, the air rushes in through a narrow tube, creating a powerful suction that pulls dust and dirt into the machine.

SEWING MACHINE

Crank turns rotary movement of axle into up-and-down movement of needle

The inside of a sewing machine is like a frantic factory where many things are happening at once. Axles spin, belts hum, rods clatter and the needle moves up and down with blinding speed. But behind this seeming chaos is a series of carefully designed movements, all powered by a single electric motor. In less time than it takes you to blink, a sewing machine makes a stitch, tightens it and moves the fabric forward in preparation for the next stitch.

MAKING THINGS MOVE

Sewing machines today are powered by small electric motors. (To find out more about electric motors, see page 47). The motor turns an axle, which is linked to the rest of the moving parts within the sewing machine. Devices called cranks and **cams** convert the rotational movement of the axle into the up-and-down movement of the needle.

Needle thread unwinds from reel on top of machine

Bobbin with thread

Connecting rod turns axle connected to toothed plate

Metal foot holds fabric down while it is being stitched

Toothed plate lifts the fabric and moves it on after each stitch

MAKING A STITCH

Spool of thread

Axle

(1) (2) (3) (4) (5) (6)

Needle thread forms upper part of each stitch

Bobbin thread forms lower part of each stitch

Bobbin hook pushes needle thread around bobbin

A sewing machine uses two threads to make a stitch. The needle thread (red), is threaded through the eye of the needle (1). When the needle moves down, the thread is pushed through the fabric, forming a loop beneath it (2). A rotating hook then catches the loop (3) and pushes it around a small reel that contains the bobbin thread (white) (4). When the needle lifts up (5), the thread is pulled tight, with the bobbin thread – now running through the loop – preventing the needle thread from being pulled from the cloth (6). The stitch is now complete.

TIGHTENING UP

Before the thread reaches the needle, it travels between two coin-shaped friction plates. These adjustable plates are held together by a screw and a spring, and they control the tension of the thread – how tight or loose it is. By increasing the pressure between the plates, the stitches become tighter.

Cam moves connecting rod up and down once every time axle turns

Belt turns bobbin hook once every time needle moves up and down

43

TOILET TANK

The toilet tank is something that we see every day, but rarely look into. Inside, the tank has two simple but effective devices that make the toilet work: a float and a siphon. The float, seen on the left of this tank, ensures that the water fills to the proper level, and no higher. The siphon, in the centre, draws water into the toilet bowl in a continuous flow. Now, are you ready to take the plunge and find out what happens when you flush the toilet?

HOW A SIPHON WORKS

A siphon is a tube in which a liquid is drawn up a short distance before flowing down to a lower level. In a toilet, it's the siphon tube that carries water from the tank to the toilet bowl below. A siphon works because of suction – this is when air is removed from a space and a liquid takes its place. Water will flow continuoulsy through a siphon so long as the tube remains full of water, and the water is flowing from a higher level to a lower level. As soon as air enters the siphon, the suction is broken and the flow of water stops.

1 MAKING WATER MOVE

The toilet handle is connected to a piston (two sliding discs) inside the siphon bell. When you push on the toilet handle, a lever pulls these discs up, forcing water into the siphon tube. This provides suction, which draws the rest of the water in the tank up into the tube as well. From there, the water quickly flows down into the toilet bowl. As the tank empties, the float falls to the bottom of the tank.

Valve control arm

Siphon tube

Lifting rod attached
to lower disc

Sliding valve operated by
movement of float

Valve

Water supply pipe

Flushing
handle

Siphon bell
with two discs
inside

Downpipe

Upper siphon disc slides freely up
and down inside siphon bell

Lower siphon
disc with holes
is attached
to lifting rod

2 SELF CONTROL

Water enters the tank through a valve. The valve is
fully open when the float sits near the bottom of the
tank. As the water pours in through the open valve, the
float slowly rises, and this makes the valve gradually
close. The float and valve are set up precisely, so that
when the tank is full, the valve is completely closed.

HAIRDRYER

A hairdryer is a very simple device used by thousands of people to dry and style their hair. At the back end of the dryer, rapidly rotating fan blades pull air into the machine. The air heats up quickly as it flows over glowing electrical elements, and is then blown out of the front to dry your hair. That's all there is to it! But read on to discover the details that allow this process to work.

Air flows around motor, keeping it cool

Rotating axle carries movement from motor to fan

Incoming air is pulled into back of dryer

① PRESS FOR ACTION

To start the hairdryer, you press the control switch. It has several settings, so you can alter the speed and temperature of the air blown out.

② AIR INTAKE

The revolving blades at the back of the dryer pull in air and blow it towards the heating element. In some dryers, the blades are set at an angle, like the blades of an aeroplane propeller. As they slice through the air, they push the air forwards. In other dryers the blades are shaped like flat paddles or scoops. When these blades turn, they throw the air outwards, and this forces it forwards through the dryer.

Control switch varies the current that flows through the dryer

③ KEEPING THE MOTOR COOL

The fan at the back of the dryer draws air through the machine. The moving air helps to keep the electric motor cool by taking the heat from it.

Heat energy is transferred to flowing air

Coiled heating element

④ TURNING UP THE HEAT

Whenever electricity flows through a wire, it produces heat. More heat is generated when the electricity flows through a long, thin wire than when it flows through a short, thick one. This is why the hairdryer's coiled heating element gets red hot, but the cable supplying the dryer with electricty remains fairly cool.

THE ELECTRIC MOTOR

Inside the hairdryer's electric motor are two rectangular loops of wire at right angles to each other. These are surrounded by a magnetic field. Follow the steps to see what happens.

1 When electricity flows through one of the loops of wire, it creates a magnetic field around the wire. (You can find out more about magnetic fields on page 58.) This field reacts with the surrounding magnet, and the loop is repelled (pushed away).

2 Once the first loop has turned a certain distance, its supply of electricity is cut off. The electric current is then sent through the second loop. The pushing force makes the second loop spin around.

3 The loops are pushed around continuously when the current is on. The force of their movement creates the power to run the machine.

Magnetic field between north and south magnets

North magnet

South magnet

Contacts with electric current to supply loops

Magnetic field around the loops repels magnetic field between magnets, causing loops to spin

Battery produces electric current

SMOKE ALARM

Just as there is no smoke without fire, there is rarely a fire without smoke. Because smoke spreads very quickly, it is often the first sign that a fire has broken out.

The electric current crosses the gap between the two plates

Rising smoke interrupts the flow of the electric current

Wires carry the changing electric signals to the **microprocessor**

Detector unit

The human nose is sensitive and is good at smelling smoke – but only when it is quite near. What if a fire were to start on the other side of a shut door, or you were asleep, or you had a cold and couldn't smell the smoke? This is when a smoke detector comes in handy. As soon as it senses smoke, an alarm is triggered that blasts throughout the house.

4 ▷ RAISING THE ALARM

The real smoke detector's alarm contains a thin metal plate. When the microprocessor receives the message that there is smoke, it switches on an electric current that makes the plate vibrate very rapidly. The result is an ear-piercing sound.

Sounding the alarm

Microprocessor

3 ▷ SENSING A CHANGE

The microprocessor monitors the level of the electric current flowing between the plates. When smoke enters the detector unit, it absorbs some of the radiation given off by the metal pellet. As a result, the air becomes less ionized and the current weakens. When this happens, the microprocessor senses the change and immediately activates the alarm.

1 ▷ DETECTOR UNIT

The detector unit consists of two metal plates, about 2.5 centimetres apart, connected to a battery. The air between the plates is **ionized**, or electrically charged, by a stream of weak **radiation**. This makes it possible for a small electric current to flow between the plates. As long as the current remains steady, the detector stays silent. But as soon as smoke spreads between the plates and disrupts the current, the alarm is triggered.

In this picture, the two metal plates are shown as two five-storey towers. The current is shown as light rays crossing the gap between the two towers.

2 ▷ CHARGING THE AIR

The detector unit contains a small metal pellet that is slightly **radioactive**. This pellet gives off a constant stream of tiny particles into the surrounding air. As the particles collide with air molecules, they become charged, or ionized. Because ions conduct electricity, a small current – generated by a battery – is able to flow between the plates.

4 APPS

Smartphones come already loaded with programs called apps. These allow you to make calls, send texts, send and receive emails, keep a calendar, store a list of contacts, tell the time and do sums. You can also get apps for playing games, or to help you make music, create videos, keep a journal, paint pictures and much, much more. Many are free or cost only a few dollars to buy and download onto your smartphone.

Chat on line

Use wireless Internet

Send texts

To open an app, you just tap on its icon. This one is for sending emails.

Read news stories

Draw pictures

5 PHOTOS AND VIDEOS

A smartphone will include at least one camera, and the photos will be good enough quality to use as a desktop background on a computer. Smartphones can also shoot videos. The more expensive phones shoot HD (High Definition) video, which is as good quality as anything you'll see on TV. Some smartphones have a second camera on the same side as the main screen. This means you can make video calls that let you see the other person as you speak to them.

When you've taken a photo, it's easy to share it with friends by sending it with a text message or an email. Or you can use a free Internet photo-sharing service.

Close-up

To make part of a photo look bigger on screen, you just touch it with pinched finger and thumb, and then spread your finger and thumb apart to zoom in

Photo roll

Website

An incredible interconnected web of wireless and satellite networks, wires, and underground cables connect us to websites that appear on our screens in seconds.

Website

Poggle

Fibre-optic cables are laid under the sea bed

Fibre-optic cables run under the street

Some places are so remote that they use satellites to connect to the Internet.

For a small monthly fee, your Service Provider connects you to the Internet so you can look at websites from all over the world.

Mobile mast

Internet Service Provider

Wireless router

Where there isn't a wired or wireless connection available, your smartphone can use the network of cellular masts to connect to the Internet.

MAKING CONNECTIONS

1 CONNECTING TO THE INTERNET

When you're at home, your mobile phone and tablet usually connect to the Internet using the same wireless network as your computer, games console or TV. When there's no wireless connection available, it uses a mobile phone network (also called a **cellular network**) to let you make calls and send text messages. This isn't as fast as a wireless connection, but it still works well if you're near a mobile phone mast.

2 TEXTING AND PHONE CALLS

Whenever you make a call or send a text, your message is turned into an electrical signal. This is beamed to a nearby mobile phone mast. The mast beams the signal to the mast nearest the person you're trying to reach, and from there it's beamed down to the person's phone, which receives the signal. After that it gets turned back into the sound of your voice or the message you typed.

3 EMAILS

Just like a computer, your smartphone can send and receive emails. You can set it to play a sound or vibrate whenever a new email arrives. It will also display a little number somewhere on the home screen to show how many emails you've received that are waiting to be read.

Emails on your smartphone

USING A MOBILE PHONE

By 2015, around 2.7 billion people worldwide owned a smartphone. These amazing mobile phones – which connect to the Internet, run little programs called **apps**, play games, take photos and shoot video – are now one of the most important gadgets on the planet. So how do they work and what can you do with them?

1 OPERATING SYSTEM

All smartphones use an **operating system**. This controls all the different bits of the phone – for example the **touchscreen**, the memory where everything is stored and the processor (the 'brain' of the phone) – and makes sure they work in harmony with all the apps you use every day. The operating system also controls all the phone's electronics, so it knows to start re-charging when you plug it into the mains, or to turn the speaker off when you plug in your headphones.

2 BATTERY

The first mobile phones had batteries that were many times bigger than the phone. Often the phone was clipped to the top of the battery, which had a big carrying handle, like a lunchbox! Modern batteries are tiny, they re-charge in a couple of hours and they last all day.

3 USB CONNECTOR

A modern smartphone has a single connector attached to a Universal Serial Bus (USB) cable. When you need to re-charge your phone, all you do is plug this connector into a special type of mains plug. You can also plug the connector directly into your computer, so you can download photos from your phone and keep them safe.

Sound jack

Volume control button

App **icon** (search)

Microphone

USB connector

USB cable

Battery

Camera

Micro processors

Earpiece

6 MEMORY

Because smartphones are used to run programs called apps, take photos, shoot video and store music, they need plenty of memory to store all this information. Some phones come with a certain amount of memory, and when it's full you have to delete stuff to make space; others include a small slot where you can plug in a little card that contains more memory.

Micro SD memory card

5 VOICE CONTROL

Smartphones are now clever enough to understand voice commands. For example, you can set a reminder in your phone's calendar by saying something like "remind me to call Billy at 3:00 pm". You can also use apps that recognize voice commands – so you might say "what time does the swimming pool open?" and the phone will search the Internet for the information.

4 SIM CARD

Every phone needs a Subscriber Identity Module or SIM card, which is a little circuit board used to store all the information unique to your phone, such as your telephone number. If you take this out of the phone, it won't be able to make calls, send texts or connect to the Internet.

SIM card

TOUCHSCREEN TECHNOLOGY

While old mobile phones used little buttons to make calls and write text messages, smartphones use touchscreens. How do they know which bit of the screen you're touching? Most send a tiny electrical current from each corner of the screen and when you touch it with your finger, this interrupts the current just enough for the phone to work out whereabouts your finger is. Then, the software can do whatever it is you want it to do – open an app, type a letter, take a photo and so on. This is called a capacitive touchscreen.

LCD display layer

Flexible transparent layer

Transparent conductive layer

7 UPLOAD VIDEO

It's easy to share your videos by uploading them to the Internet. The phone usually compresses the video automatically to make it smaller, which in turn makes it faster to upload and smoother for other people to watch.

8. LOCATION SERVICES

Some apps use location services on your phone to pinpoint exactly where you are. This enables them to direct you around on foot or in a car. It's also how an app knows you want to find a cinema or place to eat that's nearby, rather than one that's on the other side of the country.

Video sharing services are usually free, but may ask you to set up an account before you use them. Like many services, you have to be old enough before you can join in.

You can turn location services on or off whenever you like

GAMES

There are many thousands of games available to play on your tablet. Many are free, and even the ones you have to pay for don't cost much. Many games are specially written for tablets, so they can use their special features – for example, steering a car by moving the tablet around in the air or swiping your finger across the screen to move a character or throw something. Many games that were favourites on computers and consoles have been re-written to run on tablets.

Enjoy moves wherever you are

WATCHING MOVIES

Tablets have bright, high definition screens make them perfect for watching movies – in on the sofa or on long car journeys. Lots of rnet services let you watch as many films and shows as you like for a monthly fee, and e are plenty of completely free video sites have millions of videos you can watch.

6 MUSIC

A smartphone is really good for listening to music on, either through headphones or plugged in to an external speaker. You can either buy music to download onto your phone, or you can **stream** music over the Internet. This is a bit like listening to the radio, except *you* get to choose what you hear rather than the programme makers. You can also use your smartphone to make music. You can buy different guitar, drum and keyboard apps for your phone that sound as good as the real thing. Use these to make your own ringtones or record tunes and songs.

Your mobile phone can run apps that sound just like real musical instruments when you play them. They sound even better on headphones!

TABLETS

A tablet is basically a big smartphone that can't make phone calls or send text messages. It can still connect to the Internet through a wireless network (in your house or maybe a coffee shop), and some can use the mobile phone network if you're out and about. Their large screen makes them more useful for doing things such as reading books, electronic magazines and comics, or watching TV shows or Internet videos. They're also better for typing up homework projects or practising your piano skills. That extra screen space makes all the difference.

As with smartphones, you use a finger to swipe the screen up and down or side to side, and tap to select an app. Tablets also know if you're holding them upright or on their side – most apps will adjust automatically and display the right way up.

that
bed
Inte
TV
the
that

SOLAR PANELS

When it comes to producing energy, the sun is in a league of its own. Just one hour of sunlight provides more energy than everyone on planet Earth uses in an entire year. Solar panels are able to convert that energy into something useful, such as a nice hot shower or an hour in front of your favourite TV show. Here's how they work.

1 ENERGY FROM THE SUN

Solar energy can be used either to heat water or to make electricity. When it's used to heat water – for baths, showers or to keep the house warm – it's called solar thermal energy. When it's used to make electricity to run our gadgets and household appliances, it's called solar voltaic energy.

Solar thermal panel

Solar voltaic panel

2 SOLAR PANELS

Both solar thermal panels and solar voltaic panels are fitted to the roof of the house on the side that gets the most sun. Most solar panels look the same, but if you see ones made up of tubes, these are definitely solar thermal panels, used to heat water.

Hot water for the bath

Many houses combine solar panels with an ordinary boiler, so you've always got hot water, even when the weather's terrible.

Hot water for the kitchen

3 GETTING PUMPED UP

To make solar thermal energy, the house needs to be fitted with a pump. This pushes a special kind of fluid around a pipe inside your house. The pipe makes a big loop that starts inside your water tank, runs up to the roof, around the solar panels and then back down to the tank again.

Water tank

Pump pushes fluid through the long loop of pipe

Side of house that gets the most sun

56

SOLAR POWER STATIONS

You don't just find solar panels on houses. There are also huge solar power stations. These use thousands of mirrors to capture sunlight and reflect it onto a central tower, called a **receiver**. Running through the receiver are pipes full of a special liquid that gets heated by the sunlight and turned into steam. This, in turn, drives a turbine (a kind of big engine) to produce electricity. The electricity travels through overhead or underground cables, and eventually reaches your house.

Receiver

Mirror

Turbine

Overhead cables attached to a pylon

Cable carrying electricity to your house

6 ...AND SOME FOR YOU

Got any solar energy to spare? If you have, you can sell it back to the power company for cash or money off your electricity bill.

The inverter converts electricity from photo voltaic solar panels into AC current

Electricity meter

Fuse box

5 SOME FOR ME...

Solar voltaic energy passes through a meter, so you can see how much solar power is being generated. It then goes through a fuse box, which handles the way electricity is distributed around the house.

Solar voltaic energy is used to power the TV, lamps and other appliances

4 FEEL THE HEAT

As it passes through the solar panels, the fluid – which starts out cold – heats up. It's then pumped out of the panels and back down to the water tank, where it heats the water so you can enjoy a shower or maybe even do the washing up! Job done, it then starts the loop all over again.

Rays of light

Electron flows into circuit

Electron crosses junction

Dislodged electron

Flow of electrons

PHOTO VOLTAIC PANELS

Here's the technical bit. Photo voltaic solar panels are made up of individual silicon cells, which have a positive layer on top and a negative layer on the bottom. This creates the conditions for an electric field – a bit like a **battery**. When sunlight, which is made up of tiny particles of light called photons, hits the cells, it agitates the electrons so they start to move. This creates electricity. But there's a catch – it's the wrong type of electricity for running TVs and toasters! So now the electricity needs to be run through a special device called an inverter. This turns it into the right type of electricity, called AC current.

57

DOORBELL

If you have ever wondered how a doorbell works, here is your chance to find out. Like many machines, it uses electricity. When a finger presses the button, electricity produces a **magnetic field** that pulls a hammer onto a bell, making the bell ring. If the bell only rang once, it wouldn't attract much attention. Luckily, this doorbell is designed to keep clanging as long as the button is depressed. The result is a noise that no-one could ignore!

1 PRESS FOR ACTION

When someone rings a doorbell, the button completes a **circuit** and electricity begins to flow.

POWER SOURCE

The doorbell is powered either by its own batteries, or by electricity from a power plant.

Switch operated by pressing bell button

Springs pull movable contact back so it touches nonmoving contact again

CREATING A MAGNETIC FIELD

When electricity passes through a metal wire, a magnetic field forms around the wire. You can see this if you surround a wire with compasses. Normally, compass needles point north, but as soon as electricity flows through the wire, the needles show a magnetic field has been created. The wire now has the qualities of a magnet, and can **attract** and **repel** metal objects.

Switch

Compasses showing a magnetic field has been created

Compasses all pointing north

Electric current off

Electric current on

Battery

Transformer

58

3 HAMMER ACTION

The doorbell has two metal **contacts**. One stays still, but the other is on a spring-loaded arm and can slide back and forth. Attached to this arm is the hammer that strikes the bell. The electric current now flows through the two metal contacts and around the **electromagnet**. This creates a magnetic field that pulls the movable contact towards the electromagnet. As the arm moves forwards, the hammer strikes the bell.

4 MAKE OR BREAK

As soon as the arm moves and the two contacts separate, the circuit is broken, the current stops flowing and the magnetic field vanishes. Springs now pull the movable contact arm back so that the two contacts touch again, the electricity flows and the process begins again.

Hammer strikes the bell

*Bell vibrates when hit by hammer and produces **sound waves***

Stationary (non-moving) contact

Movable contact attached to hammer assembly

The current travels in coils around the magnet, producing a magnetic field

Electromagnet

2 CHANGING THE VOLTAGE

The electricity flows along a wire to a transformer. This lowers, or steps down, the voltage of the electricity – the electric force that "pushes" the electrons around the circuit. Unlike a television, a doorbell needs only a low-voltage circuit.

TEMPORARY ATTRACTION

An ordinary magnet has a continuous pull, or magnetic attraction, and so would not be of much use in a doorbell. An electromagnet is different because it only pulls when electricity is flowing.

3D PRINTER

Instead of having to go to a shop every time you need something – let's say a new mug – imagine you could just call up the basic plans on your computer, make a few changes and then build the mug yourself. Well, that's exactly what you can do with a 3D printer.

First, you'll need a plan

① COMPUTER MODEL

The first thing you'll need to do is to tell the printer what it is you want to make, and this means you need a plan. The plan needs to be a proper 3D model created by special software, usually called CAD (Computer Aided Design) software. This measures every single part of whatever you want to make and turns it into a design that's perfect. There are also thousands of designs you can download for free from the Internet.

The computer then slices the plan to make a model

② PROGRAMMING IN SECTIONS

Having created the 3D model, the computer program then 'slices' it up into very thin sections. This is necessary because of the unusual way the printer works.

Power supply

The metal support moves back and forth

The print nozzle moves in every direction – forwards and backwards, left and right

The fan turns at high speed to cool the printer head

The printer head drops of heated head moves from

The printer can make almost any shape you can think of

③ PRINTER HEAD ACTION

In a normal printer, the nozzles that spray the ink onto the page move backwards and forwards across the paper in a line. In 3D printers, however, the nozzles need to move backwards and forwards, and left and right.

The plastic line moves at a steady speed

Protective casing

⑧ FINISHED MUG

If the original model plan was good, your finished mug should look like a mug bought from a shop – though it may need a lick of paint!

⑦ WASHING THE MUG

Any objects made by a 3D printer are never completely smooth. To give your model a nice, shop-bought shine, it will need to be dipped for three or four seconds in a bowl of acetone – a cleaning chemical. This is a job for grown-ups. It should always be done wearing rubber washing-up gloves, in a room with open windows and doors.

Platform moves down

3D printers don't use ink – many use plastic stored on a spool

⑥ MOVING PARTS

The printer nozzle is attached to a series of rods that allow it to glide smoothly in any direction. This means it can follow the exact shape of the 3D design created by the computer software. The model takes shape on a platform underneath the nozzle, which sprays out the plastic in layers. As each layer is completed, the platform moves down ever so slightly. Then the nozzle starts work on the next layer.

④ LOTS OF LAYERS

When most things get made, they start as a solid chunk that machines turn and grind to make into a particular shape. 3D printers don't do this. Instead they build the shape up by printing it out in really thin layers – first one, then the next, and so on.

⑤ ADDING THE PLASTIC MATERIAL

3D printers don't use ink. Instead they use many different materials, including a type of plastic. The plastic is stored on a spool – a bit like fishing line – on the side of the printer, and is fed up through a tube to the printer nozzle. The plastic is then heated up and sprayed out of the nozzle.

WEATHER REPORT

If you want to know if it will be sunny or rainy tomorrow, you can watch the weather report on TV. But how do weather forecasters know what the weather will be like? They find out by watching the weather all around the world, and then predicting how it will develop and change over the next few days.

Clouds are made from tiny drops of water that may fall as rain

Weather balloon

Radio transmitter

How rainy is it?

How windy is it?

How damp is it?

How warm is it?

Weather station

Weather office

② IN THE AIR

Weather forecasters need to know what is going on high up in the sky, as well as at ground level. Every day, hundreds of weather balloons soar up to 32 kilometres into the sky. They carry instruments that measure the weather conditions and automatically transmit the results back to base.

① WEATHER WATCHING

All around the world, weather stations measure how damp the air is, how dense it is (the air pressure), how warm it is, how much rain falls, and the speed of the wind. The stations send their findings by radio to a local weather office. The weather office gathers the information, or data, from balloons, **satellites** and local weather stations, and beams this information up to another satellite.

Global
Telecommunications
Satellite

Weather centre
receives data

4 ARE YOU RECEIVING ME?

A Global Telecommunications Satellite (GTS) receives data from all over the world and beams it back down to a main weather centre. Here, the data is fed into a powerful computer called a supercomputer. The computer prints out exactly what it thinks the next measurements will be at each weather station.

Computer
printout

3 VIEW FROM SPACE

Satellites circling Earth in space take pictures of the world below. They transmit the pictures back to a weather office on the ground. The pictures show forecasters where the clouds are and what weather patterns are developing.

5 WEATHER CHART

Next, the computer uses the data to make a chart showing what the weather will be like in each area.

The computer's predictions are sent out to all the weather offices and stations

Making the
weather chart

Radio waves

The weather
forecaster
explains the
weather map

Weather map

Watching the TV
weather report

6 TOMORROW'S WEATHER

For the TV weather report, the forecasters use the weather chart to make up a map we can all understand. Little suns mean a sunny day, clouds represent overcast skies, droplets indicate rain, and so on. Now you know whether to wear a heavy coat or shorts tomorrow!

TELEVISION

How can you visit Mars, follow your favourite sports and watch distant wildlife without even getting out of your chair? By watching television, of course! But what is the secret of television?

Camera

Mike

Studio

1 THE PICTURE

When a TV camera takes pictures of a scene, rows of tiny **photo cells** inside the camera change the pictures into electrical blips.

Picture signal

Cameras record in just three colours: red, green and blue

2 LISTEN UP

A **microphone**, or mike, records the sound. The sound, like the pictures, is recorded as a pattern of electrical blips.

3 LIVE OR RECORDED?

News reports and sports events are often sent out 'live' as they happen. Dramas are usually recorded and sent out later.

4 FROM BLIPS TO RIPPLES

The picture and sound signals are sent to a **TV transmitter**. Strong magnets turn the electrical blips in the signals into invisible ripples of energy called radio waves.

5 BROADCASTING

Sending out TV pictures and sound is called broadcasting. The radio waves spread out from the transmitter into the air. TV programmes can also be sent as electrical blips straight to your home through cables.

Changing the signals to radio waves

ROCKET LAUNCH

It's not easy getting a satellite into space. You need a lot of rocket power to get anything off the ground, whether it's only going into low Earth orbit (anything higher than 160 kilometres) or far further. And remember, it's not just the weight of the satellite that needs to be lifted, it's also the weight of the massive rocket you're using to carry the satellite, and the weight of the fuel you'll need!

1 ENGINES

Most engines rotate, but rocket engines are different – they are reaction engines. Imagine you were standing on a skateboard holding a fireman's hose that was spraying a strong jet of water. The action of the water flying out of the hose would push the skateboard along in the other direction (this is the reaction). It can take several firemen to hold a hose because the reaction is so strong! That's how rocket engines work – except they use rocket fuel, not water.

Booster engine

*Less than one minute later, the booster engines cut out and the booster package is **jettisoned***

Solid rocket boosters

Both pairs of solid rocket boosters use up their fuel during the first two minutes of flight before being jettisoned

ROCKET THRUST

Jet engines work by mixing oxygen and fuel together, and then igniting them to produce **thrust**. However, because there's no air in space, rockets have to carry their own oxygen with them in liquid form in a huge tank.

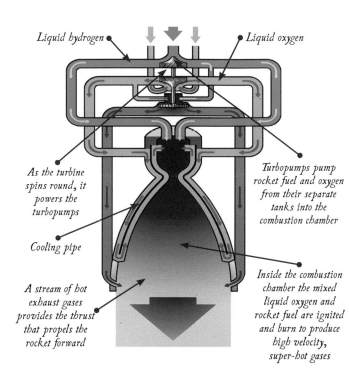

Liquid hydrogen

Liquid oxygen

As the turbine spins round, it powers the turbopumps

Cooling pipe

A stream of hot exhaust gases provides the thrust that propels the rocket forward

Turbopumps pump rocket fuel and oxygen from their separate tanks into the combustion chamber

Inside the combustion chamber the mixed liquid oxygen and rocket fuel are ignited and burn to produce high velocity, super-hot gases

2 LAUNCHING THE ROCKET

Most rockets are sent into space from a launchpad. This giant frame serves two purposes. First, it allows engineers and technicians to fill the rocket with fuel and check the outside for any problems. Second, rockets need support until they're ready for lift off. They are secured to the frame by special bolts that have a tiny explosive charge in them. When the rocket is ready to launch, these charges are set off, the bolts break and up goes the rocket.

SETTING UP A SATELLITE

There are more than 1000 satellites going around the Earth doing different jobs. Some are there to help us watch TV, others provide the SatNav in our cars, some let us talk to people in faraway places, and others help to predict the weather. Once the rocket has made it into orbit, it's time for the satellite to get to work.

COMMON TYPES OF ORBIT

There are many different types of orbit that a satellite can take around the Earth. Here are three examples.

Satellites in geostationary orbit keep pace with the Earth as it rotates, completing one orbit every 24 hours. This means they're able to stay above the same point on the Earth's surface. All geostationary satellites orbit around the Earth's equator.

Satellites in a polar orbit pass over the north and south poles. Since the Earth is rotating as the satellites complete their orbit, they're useful for mapping large areas of the Earth's surface, for example for monitoring the weather.

Satellites in low Earth orbit don't cost as much because it doesn't take as much effort to get them up there, and they can use less powerful transmitters, which are cheaper. The International Space Station is in low Earth orbit.

LOW, MEDIUM AND HIGH ORBITS

Satellite orbits are either low, medium or high. Low Earth orbit goes from about 160 to 2000 kilometres above Earth. Medium Earth orbit goes from 2000 to 35,000 kilometres, and high Earth orbit is anything above 35,000 kilometres. The Hubble Space Telescope is in a low Earth orbit and goes around the Earth every 90 minutes. **GPS satellites** (used for navigation) are in a medium Earth orbit and go around the Earth twice a day. Many satellites used to monitor the weather are in high Earth orbit and circle the Earth once a day.

Satellite

5. The upper stage then falls to Earth, where it burns up in the atmosphere.

4. Once in the correct orbit, the satellite and the upper stage separate.

3. The upper stage is now floating free, and uses its twin engines to propel itself into the correct orbit.

ALL SCRUNCHED UP

Before launch, satellites are tested on special shaking machines to see if they can handle being flung into space inside a rocket. Then they're fitted inside the rocket with their solar panels folded up to save space. When the rocket reaches the correct height above the Earth and goes into orbit, the casing around the satellite opens and falls away. This is called separation. From now on, the satellite is on its own!

UNFOLDING SOLAR PANELS

Once the satellite is in orbit, the solar panels swing out so they can capture the sun's rays and turn them into energy to power the satellite. At the same time, other instruments are unfolded. The thrusters, communications and other controls are then all tested remotely by scientists back on Earth.

Protective case

2. Once in orbit, latches open the protective case that surrounds the upper stage engine and payload, and the two parts of the case drift away.

1. The second stage propels the rocket out of the Earth's atmosphere.

ADVANCED COMMUNICATIONS SATELLITE

NASA's Advanced Communications Technology Satellite (ACTS) was launched way back in 1993. Stuffed full of technology, it was able to send electronic data (pictures, video and audio) to the remotest places on the planet at high speeds. ACTS has now been retired by NASA and is used for teaching students.

7 PICKING UP THE VIBES

An aerial picks up signals beamed straight from the TV station. TV signals bounced off satellites in space are picked up by a dish-shaped receiver.

6 TV FROM SPACE

Sometimes TV programmes have to be broadcast over a large area or to faraway places – even to the other side of the world. When this happens, the TV signal has to be bounced off a communications satellite orbiting Earth high up in space.

Radio wave

8 BLIPS AGAIN

The dish and aerial change the radio waves back into electrical blips. These go to your TV set.

9 WHAT A SHOW!

A **loudspeaker** in the TV set produces the sounds. In the TV screen, millions of tiny red, green and blue elements called pixels are controlled by the electrical signals to form the moving images. From a distance, the combinations of different pixels give the illusion of a full-colour picture.

The first stage engine continues to fire,
providing forward thrust, then finally
separates from the second stage engine

First stage engine

The upper stage engine is a miniature
version of the main engine and ignites
liquid oxygen and liquid hydrogen in a
combustion chamber to produce thrust.

4 ▸ LIQUID FUEL

The main section of most rockets is
filled with liquid fuel, which is stored
separately in two tanks. Usually one
is full of liquid oxygen and the other
contains either kerosene or liquid
hydrogen. These are pumped into
a large combustion chamber, where
they're mixed and set on fire. As they
burn, they produce gases that are
pushed out of the rocket's giant
nozzles at between 8000 and
16,000 kilometres per hour.

Solid rocket booster

First stage fuel tank

High pressure
helium bottle

3 ▸ SOLID ROCKET BOOSTERS

The solid rocket boosters are what gives
the rocket the extra 'kick' it needs to get
going from a standing start. They use
solid fuel, which is a bit like gunpowder
but has other stuff added to it so that it
burns instead of exploding. Solid fuel is
safe and is less expensive than liquid
fuel, but it has a fixed speed (it can't be
made to go faster or slower) and once
started, it can't be turned off.

Satellite (payload)

6 ▸ PAYLOAD

The payload is whatever the rocket is taking
into space in order to complete its mission.
It might be a satellite to help beam TV
programmes to anywhere in the world, or
specialized scientific equipment designed for
space experiments. It might even be a crew of
astronauts. A rocket such as this can carry
satellites that weigh as much as 6800 kilograms
(about the same as a school bus).

Upper stage
fuel tank

Upper stage
oxidiser tank

5 ▸ SECOND STAGE ENGINE

Once you've burned all the fuel in the main
tank getting off the ground and up through
the atmosphere, what happens next? The
largest part of the rocket falls away, while the
smaller bit at the top – which has an engine
and fuel of its own – starts up, pushing the
rocket further into space. Sometimes the bits
of the rocket that fall to Earth can be
recovered and used again.

Solid rocket propellant

BLAST OFF

Since 1957, Atlas rockets have
become one of the workhorses
of space exploration. They've
been the power behind
hundreds of satellite launches.
As well as delivering
commercial and military
hardware into orbit, they've
also sent the **Pioneer spacecraft**
sailing past Saturn and Jupiter
and on into the unknown.

First stage (liquid oxygen) feedline

First stage (booster) engine

Solid rocket booster nozzle

The transmitting aerial can be moved to direct transmissions to lots of destinations

Satellites in higher orbit use a microwave frequency five times higher than that used by conventional satellites for downlink transmissions

Fuel tank containing propellant to keep the satellite in exactly the right position

This ground station uses a large aerial to transmit microwave signals. Much of the data on the ground is passed in digital form through electric or fibre-optic cables.

SATELLITE DISH RECEIVER

In order for a satellite to do its job – whether it's predicting the weather, beaming a TV signal around the world or helping you get from A to B in your car – it needs to be part of a network of transmitters and receivers. These giant dishes, called parabolic antennae, communicate with satellites in low orbit using radio waves, and reach those in higher orbits using microwaves, which have a higher frequency and are better able to get through the Earth's atmosphere.

GROUND STATION

Satellite dish receivers are also called ground stations. They are usually connected to national communications networks in one of two ways. They either use fibre-optic cables that run underground or they use overland microwave radio links. This chain of transmitter-to-satellite-to-receiver is the backbone of our modern communications system.

Photovoltaic cells in the solar panels provide electricity for the communications systems

The transponder in the main body of the satellite boosts microwave signals before routing them to the transmission aerial

Battery pack stores energy collected by solar panels

Thrusters help keep the satellite in its orbit. They can move it in any direction.

Long-distance transmissions are sent around the world via a network of space satellites

The receiving aerial collects incoming microwave signals

MOTOR CAR

You probably see hundreds of cars every single day – there are more than one billion in the world – but have you ever stopped to think about how they work and the technology used inside them? Here we reveal the insides of one of the most popular, and best loved, machines of all time.

1 FOUR CYLINDER ENGINE

A car engine needs air and fuel to work. Mixing the two in a small space and adding a spark produces enough energy to move four sets of pistons up and down. These pistons are attached to a pole called a crank shaft, which in turn drives a much longer prop (propeller) shaft that runs through the middle of the car. As the pistons go up and down, they turn the prop shaft.

2 PROP SHAFT AND DIFFERENTIAL

The prop shaft needs to be able to turn the rear axle. It does this using a fancy gearing device. This device, called the differential, is also able to turn the back wheels at different speeds, so the car can go round corners smoothly.

3 GEARBOX

The gearbox does two things. Its first job is to connect and disconnect the engine and the wheels, so you can sit in traffic without the car moving. Second, there's a limit to the number of times a car engine can turn the crank shaft in a minute, so the gears are used to control this and strike the right balance between the number of times the engine turns and the speed you want the car to go. The gearbox is controlled by a gear stick and a pedal called a clutch. To break the connection between the engine and the wheels, you push down the clutch with your foot. Then you change gear and release the pedal, and the car will use the new gear.

Radiator

Four cylinder engine

Battery

Shock absorber

Brake fluid pipe

Gearbox

Fan belt

Fan

Electric motor

Brake pedal

Accelerator pedal

72

4 FUEL TANK

When you fill up with fuel, the fuel goes into a tank, and from there it's pumped to the engine. In some vehicles the pump is at the front of the car and is powered by the engine. In others it's inside the fuel tank, and runs off the car battery.

5 HYBRID BATTERY

Some modern cars use both an ordinary engine and an electric motor. The electric motor sits between the engine and the hybrid battery, and converts some of the energy produced by the engine into electricity, which is stored in the hybrid battery. When you brake, the electric motor runs backwards, which not only slows the car but also generates even more electricity.

6 EXHAUST AND CATALYTIC CONVERTER

A series of pipes runs from the engine all the way to the back of the car. It takes all the nasty gases from the engine and runs them through a catalytic converter – a box coated with chemicals. This helps to remove some of the harmful gases, such as carbon monoxide, before shooting them out of the exhaust pipe.

Brake fluid pipe – pressure applied to the brake pedal delivers hydraulic brake fluid to operate the brake discs

Fuel tank

Hybrid battery

Silencer

Exhaust pipe

Steering wheel

Handbrake

Catalytic convertor

Driveshaft

Differential

Recharging port

Brake pads

Brake discs

FOUR STROKE CYCLE

A car engine runs by letting off hundreds of tiny explosions every minute in what's called the four stroke cycle. Here's how it works.

(1) (2) (3) (4)

1. **The intake stroke** – the intake valve opens, the piston drops and the space above it fills with air and fuel.

2. **The compression stroke** – the intake valve closes so the air can't escape and the piston moves back up, squeezing the air and fuel mixture.

3. **The combustion stroke** – a spark lights the mixture to make a little explosion, which forces the piston back down.

4. **The exhaust stroke** – as the piston reaches the bottom, the outlet valve opens and gases left over after the explosion leave the chamber. The piston moves back to the top and the whole thing starts again.

73

JET AIRCRAFT

A fully loaded jet plane such as this one weighs about 24,500 kilograms. So how do you get all that weight up in the air safely and then make it go where you want it to go?

4 WINGLETS FOR STABILITY

The wings of this plane look as if a giant has taken the tips of them and bent them up. The bent bits are called winglets. You don't see them on every plane, but their job is to reduce **drag** around the wing and increase **lift**. They also help the plane to keep its balance. All of this means it can fly further on the same amount of fuel.

Some air is sucked into the chamber and compressed to increase thrust

Aerodynamic nose

High visibility cockpit

3 AERODYNAMIC COCKPIT

When a plane is flying, it spends all its time pushing air out of the way. Since planes fly forwards, it's the nose and the cockpit of the plane that are first to push against all this air. To make the air flow around them more freely and reduce **resistance**, the plane is specially designed so that it is narrower near the nose.

Less air pressure

Winglet

More air pressure

2 AIR PRESSURE CAUSES LIFT

Wings are flat on the bottom and curved on the top. As the plane flies along, air passes over and under the wing, but because the air has further to go when it passes over the wing, this air has to travel more quickly. More speed over the wing means less **air pressure** on top compared with underneath. This produces **lift**, which helps keep the plane in the sky.

5 FLAPS ON WINGS

Once in the air, you need to be able to steer the plane left and right, and up and down. Pilots use the controls in the cockpit to move the various flaps on each wing; when the pilot turns the controls to the left, the flap on the left wing goes up and the one on the right wing goes down. Since a raised flap reduces lift and a lowered flap increases it, the plane will start to roll to the left and then turn in that direction.

To ascend, pull backwards on the stick to raise the tail flap. Tail goes down, nose goes up.

To start turning, roll the plane in the direction you want to go — in this case to the left.

To descend, push forward on the stick to lower the tail flap. Tail goes up, nose goes down.

Some air is sucked in and bypasses the combustion chamber

Tail rudder

Combustion chamber

Fan

Stationary blades make engine more efficient

Cool air bypasses engine and makes up three-quarters of total thrust.

Turbines drive the front fan and internal compressors

Driveshaft

Hot gases turn the turbines and are then pushed out the back of the engine

1 JET ENGINE

Air gets sucked into the front of the engine by a series of large fans. Some of this air bypasses the main workings and goes straight out of the back of the engine. The remainder is compressed to increase its pressure, and then mixed with jet fuel in a part of the engine called a combustion chamber. Add a spark, and when the mixture catches light it expands and shoots out of the back, pushing the plane forwards. This type is called a turbofan engine, and is much quieter than other kinds of jet engines.

6 TAIL RUDDER

Unlike a boat, the rudder on a jet plane isn't used to steer it. Instead, it's used to prevent the plane from swinging to left and right while it travels in a straight line. This movement is called yaw.

SUBMERSIBLE

There are places in the ocean so deep that if you dropped Mount Everest into them, its summit (at 8848 m) would still be 1.6 kilometres – one whole mile – underwater! Exploring these dark and mysterious depths requires a special kind of submarine, called a deep sea submersible.

1 LIGHTS

Why do you need searchlights? Because below about 200 metres, light from the sun starts to fade and by 300 metres it's really hard to see anything. Below 300 metres the only light you can see comes from sea creatures.

Camera is controlled by the pilot

2 DOME

Domes give the crew a fantastic opportunity to spot underwater wildlife and other interesting features. They can't be made from glass because glass would crack under the pressure of all that water. Instead they're made from a tough, see-through plastic called acrylic, which is lighter than glass and up to 17 times stronger.

Powerful, movable lights

3 FRAME

The hull or frame of the submersible is often made from a titanium alloy – a mix of metals that is very tough, doesn't rust and is more flexible than steel, so it can handle the pressure from all that sea water without buckling. Some submersibles use other light, tough and flexible materials, such as carbon fibre – also used for making fishing rods.

Mesh basket for storing samples

4 HYDRAULIC MANIPULATOR ARMS

Since it's impossible for the people inside the submersible – called submariners – to go outside if they want to take something interesting back to the surface, many submersibles are fitted with flexible robot arms for picking up stuff. These are controlled from inside, a bit like a claw crane game at a funfair.

Remote controlled robot arm

5 STORAGE RACK

Anything picked up with the robot arm can't just be brought inside through an open window. Instead, it must be dropped into a big, open-mouthed basket, where it'll stay safe until the sub surfaces.

Levers help control
the vehicle

The circular cockpit ensures that
the pilot has a great view

Some submersibles
have room for more
than one pilot

7 THRUSTERS

Powered by electric motors, the thrusters are used to move the
submersible through the water. By adjusting the
direction in which they point, the pilot can make
the sub move up, down, backwards and
forwards. Submersibles use electric
motors because they're very
efficient – about 80 per cent
of the electricity put into
them is turned into
movement. With a
petrol engine, it's less
than 25 per cent.

Movable thrusters move
the sub in any direction

Battery

6 BATTERIES

The batteries on board a submersible
are there to make the engines go and to
provide the electricity the craft needs to run
everything else – lights, electronic equipment, life
support, the big manipulator arms that stick out of the
front, and so on. They're usually lithium ion batteries, like the
ones in your smartphone or laptop – but much bigger.

Aquanauts stay underwater outside the vehicle

Submariners pilot the submersible or work inside it

77

GLOSSARY

air pressure How thick or dense the air is. High-pressure air is thick; low-pressure air is thin.

app Short for 'application', an app is a small program that runs on a smartphone or tablet.

atoms The smallest complete particles of any solid, liquid or gas. Atoms make up everything, from the air we breathe to the machines we use.

attract To pull something without actually touching it.

axle A rotating rod. Axles are used to turn wheels or to carry movement from one place to another.

bacteria Tiny living cells. 'Good' bacteria help us in all kinds of ways, but 'bad' bacteria, or germs, can make us very ill.

battery A cell that stores electricity by turning it into chemical energy.

bearing A part of a machine that reduces friction. Bearings separate moving surfaces, and they roll, so one surface can slide past another.

cam A device shaped like a lopsided wheel that changes rotary (round and round) movement into up and down movement. A cam is mounted on a rotating shaft.

cellular network A mobile phone or wireless network that divides an area of land into sections or 'cells'. Each cell has a base station, used for connecting mobile phones to the telephone network.

circuit A loop that has no open ends. Electrical circuits can be very short or many miles long.

compressor A device that squeezes (compresses) a liquid or a gas, forcing it into a small space.

condense To turn from a gas or a vapour into a liquid. Gases and vapours condense either when they are cooled, or when they are compressed.

contact (electrical) Something that is designed to complete a circuit so that electricity can flow. Most electrical contacts are made of metal.

current (electric) A stream of moving particles, called electrons, that carry energy. When an electric current is switched on, energy can travel a huge distance almost instantly.

drag The force that planes push against so they can move forward. Drag is why planes need engines.

electricity A form of energy that is carried through wires.

electromagnet A magnet that works because of electricity. Unlike permanent magnets, electromagnets only work when electricity flows through them.

electron A tiny particle that carries a negative electric charge. Electrons linked together make up an electrical current. All atoms contain electrons.

enzyme A substance that speeds up a chemical reaction thousands or millions of times.

evaporate To turn into a vapour. Water slowly evaporates if it is left in a dry place.

ferment The process by which yeast helps sugar to split into alcohol and carbon dioxide gas.

filter bed Layers of sand and small stones covered by bacteria that clean dirty water trickling through them.

flocs Clumps of dirt that form when water is cleaned.

friction A force that slows down a moving object. Friction can be reduced by using oil or bearings, but it can never be stopped altogether.

fuse A safety device that stops an electric current from flowing if too much electricity is being used.

gear A toothed wheel designed to transfer movement. Gears turn each other by their interlocking teeth, and they can be used to change a movement's speed, force, or direction.

generator A machine that makes an electric current using a coil of copper wire spinning between the poles of a large magnet.

GPS satellites About 30 Global Positioning Satellites go round the Earth 'pinging' billions of devices, such as phones and car SATNAVs, so you know exactly where you are.

hydroelectric station Place where electricity is made when a generator is turned by the force of moving water.

icon A little picture on a computer or smartphone screen that represents an app or other program, an option (choice) or a window.

incinerator A very hot oven where rubbish is burned.

insulating Blocking the path of heat or electricity. Plastics, glass, ceramics and rubber are insulating materials.

ionized Made up by ions. Ions are atoms that have gained or lost electrons. Unlike atoms, they have an electrical charge.

jettisoned Deliberately dropped from an aircraft or spacecraft in flight.

lift The upward force that keeps an aircraft in the air. Lift is created by differences in air pressure.

loudspeaker A device that changes an electric current into sound.

magnet A piece of metal (usually steel) that pulls other metals towards it or pushes them away with an invisible force called magnetism. Magnets can also move electrons through metal wires.

magnetic field An invisible region around a magnet in which its effects can be felt. The field is strongest in the area closest to the magnet.

mains Underground pipes or cables that carry water, electricity or gas to your home.

meter A device that measures how much water, gas or electricity you use.

microphone A device that changes the vibrations of sound (such as voice) into an electric current.

microprocessor An electronic device that carries out calculations. Microprocessors are at the heart of all computers and calculators.

microwaves Tiny pulses of energy that can carry a phone call to a satellite and back, or heat up a meal.

molecule A chemical unit, such as water, which is made up of two or more atoms that are linked together.

nozzle A funnel-shaped opening, narrow end pointing outwards, at the end of a pipe or tube. A liquid or gas speeds up when it passes through a nozzle, and expands when it leaves it.

nuclear fuel Fuel, such as uranium, that can be used in nuclear reactors as a source of electricity.

operating system An electronic 'conductor' that makes sure all the parts of a computer – hardware and software – work together in harmony.

optical character reader An electronic computer eye that can read both letters and numbers.

orbit The curved path a spacecraft takes around a planet or moon.

photo cell A device that changes the light coming into a TV camera into electrical blips.

Pioneer spacecraft A series of American robot spacecraft sent to observe the Sun, Jupiter, Saturn and Venus. Pioneer 10 is now more than 12 billion kilometres from Earth.

postcode A code for a street used by computer sorting systems.

pressure The force with which things press against their surroundings. The pressure of a gas or vapour can be increased by heating it up.

radiation A form of energy that spreads out from an object. Light is a form of radiation.

radioactive Giving off radiation. Some radioactive substances are dangerous because their radiation can harm living things.

radio waves Invisible pulses of energy that spread TV or radio signals through the air.

receiver A device that picks up incoming signals. Televisions, radios and telephones all have receivers.

recycled Waste materials that have been used to make new things.

repel To push something away without actually touching it. Magnets repel each other if their matching poles are lined up.

reservoir A natural or artificial lake or pond, or an underground cavern, used for storing water.

resistance An opposing force.

satellite A pilotless spacecraft that circles, or orbits, the Earth.

sedimentation tank A container in which dirty water is left to stand so lumps of dirt can sink to the bottom.

sewer A huge drain for waste water and sewage.

sizing machine A machine that sorts letters according to their size.

sludge The mud that settles out of sewage or dirty water.

sludge digestion tank A container in which bacteria eat the sludge removed from sewage.

sound wave Waves of pressure that carry sound. Both in ears and microphones, these waves are converted into movement.

stream A continous flow of music or video received over the Internet.

suction Removing air from a space in order to force a liquid (or, in the case of a vacuum cleaner, different air) into that space.

threshing A process that shakes out the grains from harvested wheat.

thrust The force that moves an aircraft through the air. Engines produce thrust.

touchscreen A screen on a smartphone or tablet that allows you to choose things, or change the size of pictures, just by touching the screen.

transformer A device that makes an electric current stronger or weaker.

transmitter A device that sends out TV, radio or telephone signals.

transponder Electrical device on a satellite designed to receive a specific signal and automatically transmit a specific reply.

turbine A special wheel with slanting blades. Wind, water or steam rushes past the turbine and pushes on the blades. This spins the wheel so that it drives a generator.

valve A device that lets something flow in one direction, but not in another. Valves are often found in machines that pump liquids or gases.

vapour A gas that has been formed by the evaporation of a liquid.

winnowing Separating wheat grains from their husks.

79

INDEX